Ever Ascending: The Resurrection Series

THE LAST ADAM

L. Emerson Ferrell

Voice Of The Light Ministries

The Last Adam
Ever Ascending: The Resurrection Series, Vol. 1
© 2014 L. Emerson Ferrell, 4th Edition 2015

Category: Reformation

Published by: Voice Of The Light Ministries
                   P.O. Box 3418
                   Ponte Vedra, Florida 32004
                   www.voiceofthelight.com

Printed: United States of America

ISBN 10:   1-933163-74-7
ISBN 13:   978-1-933163-74-1

TABLE OF CONTENT

EVER ASCENDING
THE RESURRECTION SERIES

My life changed dramatically after I confronted what I believed with why I believed it. That started a journey in my life that's constantly moving upward or as the title describes, ever ascending.

My journey began when the Holy Spirit explained the conversation between Christ and Mary, after His resurrection.

Jesus said to her, "Woman, why are you weeping? Who are you looking for?" She, supposing him to be the gardener, said to him, "Sir, if you have carried him away, tell me where you have laid him, and I will take him away."

Jesus said to her, "Mary." She turned and said to him, "Rabboni!" which is to say, "Teacher!"

Jesus said to her, "Don't touch me, for I haven't yet ascended to my Father; but go to my brothers, and tell them, 'I am ascending to my Father and your Father, to my God and your God.'"
John 20:15-17

Jesus knew the answer to each question He ever asked. Therefore, because of His great love for the people He would expose them to their greatest fears by asking the questions they were afraid to face.

The two questions He asked her are obvious to Him, but too painful for Mary. "Why are you weeping? Who are you looking for?" Unfortunately, Mary's behavior demonstrates the condition of the modern day church. She was crying because she thought He was dead. She was coming to anoint a dead corpse with the spices she had prepared.

The last thing anyone should be doing is crying. Mary should have been rejoicing because the promised One had come and done what was prophesied from Genesis. The truth is none of His followers believed what the resurrected Christ had accomplished. They were living in the most remarkable time in all of history, but without spiritual understanding it could have felt like the end of the world.

The second question He asks her is as relevant today as it was in her time. "Who are you looking for?" Sadly, today just like then, people don't really know "who they are looking for" because religion has trained us with images and stories that don't describe the resurrected Christ. The Jewish leaders expected Him to conform to their understanding that was void of the spiritual ways and nature of their Creator. All religions are formed and depend on their understanding, not that of the Spirit.

Are you like Mary? Do you find yourself in that same situation? If so, I encourage you to read these books with an open heart. Then have the courage and faith to trust the Holy Spirit to remove every obstacle from your mind that will prevent your seeing the risen Christ in all His glory.

Jesus told Mary not to cling to Him because He knew by her response that she didn't recognize Him as the Christ. Jesus fulfilled His assignment as the Lamb of God and resurrected as our Royal High Priest from the order of Melchizedek. Unless we experience a spiritual rebirth it will be impossible to understand the authority and majesty in that Priestly Order.

These books will offer a fresh Biblical approach to the completed work of Christ in a life-empowering way that will alter your future and that of the next generations.

Be prepared for these books to encourage, inspire and provoke you to higher dimensions of Him. You will be challenged to examine the foundation of your Christianity. For example, ask yourself, "Is my belief and or relationship with Christ formed by my revelation or another person's revelation?"

Each of these books from this Resurrection Series is written from deep experiences with the Spirit of Truth. They are written to those with the courage to invite the Holy Spirit to correct, inspire or replace their current mindset. Is that you?

You have what it takes to break out of traditions and wrong thinking to hear directly and consistently from the Holy Spirit. The day that happens it will never stop and that river of living water will gush from you with greater and greater revelations of Christ.

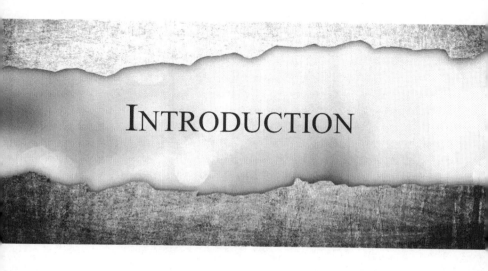

INTRODUCTION

Have you ever experienced waking from a deep sleep and for an instant not knowing where you are? Suddenly, the next several minutes are spent frantically reassuring yourself of your location and your sanity. But suppose that helplessness is your first step to discovering your power over fear and death.

The Last Adam is more than just the title of a book. It describes the resurrected Christ and His completed work.

The love story between God and man is so spectacular and complete that after reading this book you will fall in love with Jesus all over again.

The first Adam was perhaps the most magnificent specimen ever created because his authority and purpose over planet earth required it. He was placed in the Garden of Eden as the steward over the physical and spiritual dimensions of this planet. His failure was catastrophic because the virus of sin and death entered the earth and has been perpetuated through his bloodline even today.

Nevertheless, what appeared to be satan's triumphant conquest at the cross became his complete and utter destruction. The cross and resurrection were just the beginning of the majestic return of the Garden of Eden. However, because of the finished work of the last Adam the name has been changed to God's kingdom.

And so it is said, the first man Adam was a living soul.
The last Adam is a life-giving spirit.
1 Corinthians 15:45 BBE

In order to see and understand this kingdom you must be reborn. It's this rebirth that this book describes with clarity and compassion because we have all been misled. Understanding that salvation is the beginning and not the end to God's promises is the crucial purpose for this book. You will discover that the power of the "new birth" is both available and paramount for anyone who wants an *ever ascending* revelation of Christ.

The experience Jesus describes to Nicodemus can only occur through an immersion in Christ as the Water and Spirit. That birth will remind you of those encounters of waking to an unfamiliar place. This time, however, you will never want to leave. The joy and peace of "knowing" without learning is the dimension of Christ that will change the way you think. That place is the kingdom of God and this book will open your spiritual eyes to its reality and location.

CHAPTER 1
ADAM'S BLOOD

The blood in our veins not only keeps us alive, but originated in heaven. That's a bold statement unless you understand the complexity of this marvelous liquid that's both the origin of life and the substance that sustains it. Even though science can make synthetic blood it won't reproduce life. It will only transport oxygen to the cells for a limited time.

The first Adam was created with God's blood. The *last Adam* was born with it because His mother was impregnated from heaven. Sin, however, is a spiritual virus that corrupts man's blood, which both separates us from God while also destroying our bodies and souls.

Therefore, God determined that blood would be the only acceptable restitution for sin and required it for mankind's redemption.

Blood is not just the source of all life, but it also transmits our thoughts and imaginations throughout our "bloodlines" or generations. Adam's blood was so pure that he could live forever and control all of his thoughts. I believe he was created with more mental power than any computer man can make today.

Imagine waking up each day free from fear, pain, anxiety or tormenting thoughts. For most people this would be too good to be true. Yet, Adam experienced that kind of freedom in the Garden of Eden. The beauty and splendor of the planet during that time was literally heaven on earth. The smells and sounds of nature were in harmony with man and his Creator.

One example of this is found in Genesis when God separated light and darkness. The days on earth were separated by evening and morning, not by darkness. God walked with man in the cool of the evening, but sin entered and separated man so far from God that darkness was the result. And that darkness was both physical and spiritual.

The Perfect Blood

Genesis describes the way the first Adam was made and his purpose.

> *Then God said, "Let Us make man in Our image,*
> *according to Our likeness; let them have dominion over*
> *the fish of the sea, over the birds of the air, and over the*
> *cattle, over all the earth and over every creeping*
> *thing that creeps on the earth."*
> *Genesis 1:26*

The words "image" and "likeness" are used to remind man of His origin and nature. Likeness is used in the epistle to the Romans and explains the power of that word.

> *For if we have been united together in the likeness*
> *of His death, certainly we also shall be in the*
> *likeness of His resurrection,*
> *Romans 6:5*

The *last Adam* is the life giving spirit because He carried the blood of His Father. The verse in Romans describes the process to receive that powerful transfusion. The rebirth is the only way that will occur and Jesus is both the source and model for that transition.

The first Adam was surrounded in glory and designed for ruling both the physical and spiritual dimension. He walked and spoke with God daily. Time was irrelevant because death was neither a word nor a reality on earth.

The first Adam dominated the physical universe because his spirit was connected to his Father. The same can be true today with our physical bodies once our spirit is reconnected to the Spirit of God. **The importance of understanding the first Adam's authority and power will reveal the devastating effects sin created.**

More significantly it will emphasize the importance of what the completed work of Christ brought back for those who are "born into Him."

The first Adam was the magnificent specimen of mankind created by God and placed in His kingdom called the Garden of Eden. His physical and mental capacity was unlimited as long as he was connected to the Spirit of God. The soul is the spiritual apparatus created to bridge between the physical and spiritual being of man. It's the home to our mental and emotional centers. It was originally designed to submit to man's spirit, but sin severed that connection and resulted in man becoming a self-centered being.

Very simply, you have a soul; you live in a body; and you are a spirit. Before sin man lived in harmony with the material world because his spirit was connected to God.

I remember learning some valuable lessons with a group of Believers who identified themselves as the "word of faith group." Anyone familiar with the Bible understands the power of faith and the spoken word. I remember listening to awesome testimonies of those who received miracles in the form of healings and deliverances.

My association with that group caused me to speak differently concerning my circumstances. For instance, I wouldn't talk about pain, discomfort or sickness. I was taught to quote the scripture in Romans that says, (paraphrasing) *calling things that are not as though they were.* That awareness made me conscious of just how corrupted my bloodline and mindset were from birth.

The greatest lesson I've learned about this is that confessing scripture can change circumstances, but only a "new birth" can change mindsets.

The Power of Names

Adam was created with such power that his voice carried a frequency of faith that caused the material world to respond. The power in his voice and the word he spoke gave the animals both their character and purpose. He spoke and instantly the attributes of the creature he was observing were transmitted from the invisible to the physical realm.
The material world was his to reproduce after the images from his heart, mind and voice.

Adam named all the animals of the earth including the serpent that deceived Eve. Did you ever wonder why satan chose that creature to deceive man? Perhaps, he waited until after Adam named it before making that decision because he knew the name meant shrewd or cunning. He also knew that all the animals he named prior to the serpent adopted the behavior of their names.

In a sense Adam was a co-creator with God to produce on earth as it was in heaven. That was a monumental assignment and a task that he was physically, mentally and spiritually created to perform.

But sin perverted the soul of man and his heart was captured by evil rather than good. Remember, God warned Adam not to eat of the tree of the knowledge of good and evil. That's why assigning a name to a condition or situation gives life to the character or nature of that name. This is especially evident when a doctor diagnosis diseases. The diagnosis has no life without a person's belief.

*"Then the LORD heard the voice of your words when you spoke to me, and the LORD said to me: 'I have heard the voice of the words of this people which they have spoken to you. They are right in all that they have spoken. **Oh, that they had such a heart** in them that they would fear Me and always keep all My commandments, that it might be well with them and with their children forever!"*
Deuteronomy 5:28, 29

This scripture in Deuteronomy demonstrates the difference between speaking from the soul or the heart. God knows the frequency of the heart is different from that of the mind.

When man's heart is connected to God's Spirit the way Adam's was created it has power to alter the physical realm. His words carried a resonance and a frequency we call faith. This is worth repeating: The first Adam believed God and his voice vibrated with the resonance of faith, which is capable of changing the molecular structures of the material world. That's the same way God created the universe.

Bible faith is different than the faith we use each day. For example, most people believe that objects resembling a chair will support their weight if they sit in it. The same kind of trust is transmitted to people whose opinions we believe, such as a doctor.

If a doctor diagnosis a patient with cancer that person, because of a sin mindset will imagine death and releases fear. Mind you, all the doctor had to do was to tell the patient they had cancer. The mind of that patient receives the suggestion the same way the earth receives a seed. Fear is the seed that will eventually destroy anyone who receives it.

Cancer is only a name until we give it life with our belief. The life we lead is determined by what we believe. Remember, Adam had dominion over what he named before he sinned, not afterwards. But man believes if he names a disease or some other problem he will have superiority over the condition. That's different than controlling or changing it. You can only control what you have dominion over. Sin, sickness and disease are the fruit of lies and deception. They originated with satan and were passed into the bloodline of the first Adam through sin.

Fear is the substance of satan and his power to steal, kill and destroy is derived by making creatures believe lies. The Bible says he is the father of lies and therefore he will reproduce after his kind.

Faith is the substance of God and it reproduces the fruit of His Spirit, which is mainly life, dominion and abundance. If you trust in Him you will live, but if you trust fear you will die.

The cycle of fear begins before people go to a doctor when they respond to the voices of fear in their bodies identified by "symptoms." Fear is the reason for going to the doctor in the first place. Once that door is opened it usually takes a miracle to close it.

Corrupted Bloodlines

We see the masterpiece of God in the way He created the first Adam. Man without limits in his body, mind or spirit had the power to rule and reign over all creation and all the animals were subject to him. His imagination and his power to conceive and to create inventions were limitless. All of this was engrafted in his DNA to be passed to each generation. But sin entered the picture and the immediate result was Cain murdering Abel œ producing the blood shedding that has never stopped.

Adam's offspring were endowed with a consciousness and imagination as powerful as his. The glorious gifts that God gave to the first Adam were now in the wrong hands and manipulated by the wrong spirit because of sin. The perversion produced by the fall was so sinister that it influenced even angels.

Genesis mentions "sons of god" committing sexual sins with the women on earth. Some believe this refers to angels, but what's important to me was the result of that intercourse. God had to destroy and utterly wipe out all life on earth with a flood because of the race of giants produced from that sin. Noah and his family were the only ones to survive the flood, but the blood was still from the first Adam.

The consciousness of sin is transmitted through our bloodline affecting everything including our thoughts and beliefs. Therefore, sin was passed to the generations of Noah even though the flood destroyed all physical life.

The first Adam's blood and DNA was God's. It carried so much power and life that many of his descendants lived over 700 years. God told Noah that the thoughts of man were evil from birth and that's what forced God to set a lifespan of 120 years.

Consequently, man has a limited time to experience Christ and to discover the truth and power of the *last Adam*. The following verses indicate the fallen condition of man after the first Adam and they give the only solution made possible through Christ.

And the LORD said, "My Spirit shall not strive with man forever, for he is indeed flesh; yet his days shall be one hundred and twenty years."
Genesis 6:3

Then the LORD saw that the wickedness of man was
great in the earth, and that every intent of the thoughts
of his heart was only evil continually.
Genesis 6:5

For just as [because of their union of nature] in Adam all
people die, so also [by virtue of their union of nature]
shall all in Christ be made alive.
1 Corinthians 15:22 AMP

Those who remain "in Adam" will die spiritually because they didn't submit to God's Spirit. Man is born "in Adam" meaning his foundation or his beliefs and decisions are made from the corrupted soul of sin. The soul is where our minds determine whom and what to believe. The first Adam chose to trust the created over the Creator, which is why he lost his spiritual authority and access to God.

A man is either redeemed or condemned by his blood that sustains his physical life and spiritual destiny.

For the life of the flesh is in the blood, and I have given it
to you upon the altar to make atonement for your souls; for
it is the blood that makes atonement for the soul.'
Leviticus 17:11

Our blood both nourishes and creates our cells with the energy or electromagnetic power to attract heaven or hell into our thoughts. It's from these thoughts that we choose our destiny and course as either sons of the first or the last Adam.

Life-Giving Spirit

*And so it is written, "The first man Adam became a living being." **The last Adam became a life-giving spirit.***
1 Corinthians 15:45

Adam's bloodline could no longer be used to reproduce sons of God. But God had a plan before the foundation of the world that would redeem His creation and complete His work. Jesus, the last Adam carried and shed His blood for the salvation of all men. His blood also reopened the door to His kingdom on earth.

The *last Adam*, Christ Jesus, restored mankind back to His Father through "His blood," which was God's blood. Jesus' blood is so powerful that anyone who calls on His name will be saved.

His sacrifice was sufficient to save all mankind from eternal separation from God.

For there is no distinction between Jew and Greek, for the same Lord over all is rich to all who call upon Him. For "whoever calls on the name of the LORD shall be saved."
Romans 10:12, 13

Although salvation will save a man's soul from eternal separation from God it does nothing to alter his desire for darkness over light. We've found Believers that have recited the "sinner's prayer," but are addicted to pornography, fornication or other perversions.

The heart can't be converted until it has received a blood transfusion from the "life-giving" Spirit. That's only achieved by a rebirth into the Spirit of Christ.

All things were made through Him, and without Him nothing was made that was made. In Him was life, and the life was the light of men.
John 1:3, 4

This verse defines the difference between "things" and life or light. The material world consists of things. Jesus told the disciples in the Book of Matthew that God knows that you need "things," but they would come to those who seek first God's kingdom. We will learn later that Jesus is the kingdom of God. The blood Jesus carried was both light and life. His sacrifice on the cross was much more than salvation. It's the door into the reality of the spiritual life as the last Adam.

And this is the judgment, that the light has come into the world, and people loved darkness rather than light because their deeds were evil. For all who do evil hate the light and do not come to the light, so that their deeds may not be exposed. But those who do what is true come to the light, so that it may be clearly seen that their deeds have been done in God."
John 3:19-21 NRSV

The scriptures above speak volumes about the power of the blood to attract either darkness or light. We are all born with the physical blood and spiritual connection from the first Adam.

That lineage compels man to the darkness and repels them from the light and unless there's a spiritual awakening by the last Adam they will die in the same darkness that attracted them.

> *But Jesus said to him, "Follow me, and let the*
> *dead bury their own dead.*
> *Matthew 8:22*

> *Jesus said to him, "Let the dead bury their own dead,*
> *but you go and preach the kingdom of God."*
> *Luke 9:60*

These verses illustrate in bold terms what most Believers often forget which is that man is a spirit being. His design is like the first Adam and that's to rule and reign with God in dominion over the material universe.

God supplied the spiritual solution for sin, but each person is responsible for entering the kingdom.

The real struggle takes place because man is deceived into thinking and believing that salvation and entering the kingdom of God are the same. They aren't the same. They are very different. Man must experience a "rebirth" to enter the kingdom of God.

> *And from the days of John the Baptist until*
> *now the kingdom of heaven suffers violence,*
> *and the violent take it by force.*
> *Matthew 11:12*

The violence Jesus speaks about is concerning the mindset and structures of the mind. Until Adam ate from the tree of "knowledge" his mind was pure, innocent and undefiled. He believed God and lived without any desire or distress. Adam's decision to disobey was more than just committing an action. It unleashed a tsunami of emotions, sensations, observations and attitudes that were both unknown and exhilarating.

It would be like children wandering through a forest of sweets like candy, pie or cakes with no restrictions or limits on what they could eat. The children would have a great time, but the consequences could be brutal. Too much of that diet could destroy them and their future generations unless there was some kind of intervention.

Righteousness demands that God give man the freedom to choose. So, man has free will because God understood that the knowledge of what makes the physical world operate without spiritual wisdom would destroy man.

If we don't understand man, the remarkable creature God made, we will never grasp the catastrophic effect of sin. The purpose of this book is to expose you to the perfect design created by God before the foundation of the world.

That perfect design includes salvation or reconciliation *and* the spiritual rebirth that places man in the original position of the first Adam.

The blood we are all born with originates from the first Adam. It's both the source of physical life and spiritual death because it contains the *spiritual virus* of sin. The first Adam demonstrated the power of that blood in many ways. I believe his naming all of the animals and reproducing offspring that lived hundreds of years are a couple of examples of that. Until sin, man's capabilities were unlimited in the physical or spiritual dimensions.

God created a son in His image and likeness with all the faculties to rule at His side. Sin entered and therefore severed man's connection with Him. However, the most majestic plan for all the ages provided Jesus as the spotless Lamb to reconcile man with His creator. God created man with "free will" because He is righteous. Man's choice to sin wasn't a surprise to Him because the plan was made before the foundation of the world.

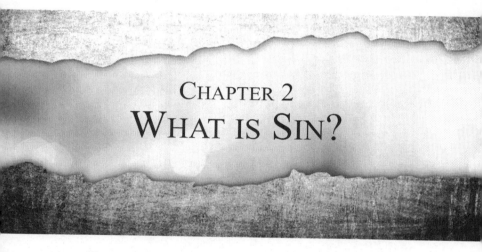

CHAPTER 2
WHAT IS SIN?

Sin is a spiritual condition of darkness, which forces our soul into a position of authority. Pride is the offspring of that condition and makes the hearts of men as stone. Man's condition requires a spiritual solution to save him from himself and to restore his relationship with God.

I have come as a Light into the world, so that whoever believes in Me [whoever cleaves to and trusts in and relies on Me] may not continue to live in darkness.
John 12:46 AMP

Christ provided the substitute for man's separation from God by sacrificing His life and blood for all mankind's condition as a result of Adam's choice. That single act by God's son destroyed all unrighteousness forever and established His Word or Light as judgment forever over darkness.

Furthermore, His blood carried the power of God to destroy sin's spiritual hold over man. His blood also provided the freedom for man to recognize and obey His creator as if the past never happened.

The weakness of man was turned into the glory of God by the work of Christ.

I first learned about sin when I was twelve years old. I was taught that all human beings are born sinners. I also learned that without repenting and turning my life over to Jesus I would go to hell. The very description of hell scared me and convicted me of my "sin."

The preacher then explained from Paul's letters to the Romans what I needed to do to be saved from hell and go to heaven. That was the beginning of my journey to know the love of God demonstrated by Christ's ultimate death and resurrection.

Christ the Overcomer

The death of Jesus on the cross and His resurrection are without question the story most people have heard and many believe.

In fact, believing that according to many teachings means you are saved and born again. I know that because it's what I was taught in the churches I attended. Nevertheless, that belief did little to change my habits, desires or goals in life.

In fact, it formed me into a type of religious Pharisee that would condemn those who didn't believe as I did. It wasn't until much later that I learned the spiritual significance of what Christ did is an *ever ascending* message that requires a rebirth to understand.

Man has free will to do as he likes, but all unrighteousness will be judged by God's love and His authority which is righteousness. Righteousness has a responsibility to protect love from sin.

The light of God contains both love and righteousness as one. Righteousness produces love and vice versa. Sin is darkness and unrighteousness and inevitably will be judged by both the righteousness and love of God. Therefore, God doesn't judge because He is angry, but because He loves.

The spiritual realm is the reality and the origin of all things and the fabric, which holds it together is love. Those who have seen angels understand that they obey God because of both His righteousness and love demonstrated by the sacrifice of His Son.

God forewarned Adam and Cain. They knew what would happen if they didn't take authority over sin.

Let's look at this warning in several translations.

If you do well, will you not be accepted?
And if you do not do well, sin lies at the door.
And its desire is for you, but you should rule over it.
Genesis 4:7

If you do well, you can hold up your head; but if not,
sin is a demon lurking at the door: his urge is toward
you, yet you can be his master."
Genesis 4:7 NAB

If you do well, won't you be accepted? But if you don't do
well, sin is lying outside your door ready to attack.
It wants to control you, but you must master it."
Genesis 4:7 GWORD

If you do well, will you not be accepted?
And if you do not do well, sin crouches at your door;
its desire is for you, but you must master it.
Genesis 4:7 AMP

Sin began with Adam and was directly passed through his bloodline to Cain. Remember, both Cain and Abel brought a sacrifice before God. Their actions were correct, but Abel's heart was righteous according to God and his offering was accepted. Sin took the form of rejection and crouched at Cain's door. He opened the door to that voice.

Jesus stands at the door and knocks today, but if all we hear is the noise generated by a soul tormented with emotional and mental fears we won't hear Him.

Behold, I stand at the door and knock. If anyone hears
My voice and opens the door, I will come in to
him and dine with him, and he with Me.
Revelation 3:20

Sin isn't what you do, but why you do it. It's the WHY that produces unbelief which is the unrighteousness that God judges. We all assume that our actions such as smoking, cursing and lying are what condemn us. But are they?

God told Hosea to marry a harlot. He gave Moses laws condemning anyone who didn't keep the Sabbath day. That day, however, was one of the only days Jesus would perform miracles. The scriptures are clear to me that God only judges the hearts of men. But religious Pharisees judge the actions of men because they are oblivious to their own darkness.

Sin is the byproduct of unbelief and the spiritual consequence is death or separation from God for eternity.

For the wages of sin is death...
Romans 6:23

Therefore, "sin" is a spiritual substance that produces death in all life because it separates man from the source of all life which is God.

In order to reverse the curse of sin God had to sacrifice righteousness for unrighteousness with His only Son. Jesus and His blood abolished Adam's sin forever.

For this purpose the Son of God was manifested, that He might destroy the works of the devil.
1 John 3:8

The work of the devil is to separate man from God through doubt and unbelief.

The kingdom of this world was formed from the tree of the knowledge of good and evil in the Garden of Eden. The consciousness of those born into Adam's bloodline is created from that sin-bearing fruit. Consciousness is the mindset produced from either the first Adam or the *last Adam*.

For God knows that in the day you eat of it your eyes will be opened, and you will be like God, knowing good and evil.
Genesis 3:5

Satan believes that power and order originate from knowledge. That's lawless according to God and it's what trapped satan. In my opinion, the tree of the knowledge of good and evil or "duality" is the mind of satan. His nature is iniquity conceived from evil or unbelief and its fruit is sin.

The tree of the knowledge of good and evil, however, operate according to laws. One of those laws demands death to anyone who kills an innocent person. Jesus was innocent and was murdered by satan thus condemning satan to death by his own law.

But there's a consequence for man. Every time man eats of that fruit decisions and choices are formed without faith. Man is incapable of living according to the Laws of God and because of this man's character is formed by disobedience and rebellion. That's why faith is the only thing that pleases God and anything else produces death.

> *...for whatever is not from faith is sin.*
> *Romans 14:23b*

All unbelief is sin and describes the condition of man who has partaken of that "tree."

Abel's death was more than murder because it introduced a word and a condition that was passed to all generations. That word was "death" and that condition was the fear of dying. Mankind lost his spiritual connection with God and he didn't understand that the consequences were far greater than the material realm.

The Second Death

The Bible speaks of another death that's not physical, but rather spiritual. This was a direct consequence of sin and the most important for mankind.

Jesus called it the "second death."

Then Death and Hades were cast into the lake of fire.
This is the second death.
Revelation 20:14

*But the cowardly, unbelieving, abominable, murderers,
sexually immoral, sorcerers, idolaters, and all liars shall
have their part in the lake which burns with fire and
brimstone, which is the second death.*
Revelation 21:8

When Jesus often spoke about death, He was describing the
second death. He understood the authority over the grave
because that's what He came to impart to those who believed
in Him. Those who misunderstand that put their trust in the
physical world instead of the spiritual realm. If Jesus
conquered anything it was the grave and the fear it has over
those who don't know or believe in Him.

The scriptures below explain the condition of man before the
Law of Moses was introduced. Our Heavenly Father wants
His creation returned. His magnificent plan is a masterpiece
designed and woven from His great love for man.

From Adam to Moses man was separated forever from God
until Jesus preached to their spirits while He was in the heart
of the earth.

Christ then preached to the spirits
that were being kept in prison.
1 Peter 3:19 CEV

For until the law sin was in the world, but sin is not
imputed when there is no law.
Romans 5:13

That sin disturbed relations with God in everything and
everyone, but the extent of the disturbance was not clear
until God spelled it out in detail to Moses.
So death, this huge abyss separating us from God,
dominated the landscape from Adam to Moses.
Romans 5:13 MESSAGE

Adam's sin separated man from God. The result was an exchange of God's image and likeness for his own. This is the image and likeness that is passed throughout all mankind. The necessary steps needed to resolve that situation began with Abraham and is completed through Christ Jesus.

The Bible says everything that's not from faith is sin. Therefore, overcoming sin demands the spiritual force of faith. It's what is needed to bring man back to God, but the design was hidden in the law to trap satan and his bloodline.

It's important to understand that Jesus used the word "death" to describe man's spiritual condition and not the end of physical life. A critical point we often overlook is that reality originates from the eternal realm, not the physical.

If we want to please God we must make choices based on faith not fear. Everything Jesus did was from His spiritual and mental authority over sin. Unless the life-giving spirit reconnects our spirit with His Spirit, our thinking won't change and neither will our image and likeness of the first Adam. That's why we must be "born again."

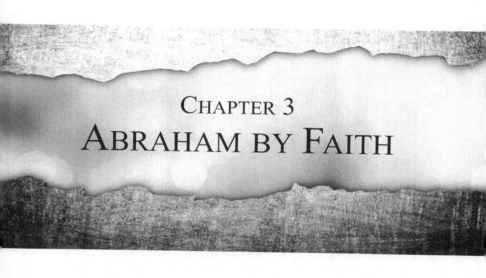

CHAPTER 3
ABRAHAM BY FAITH

Before the foundation of the world God ∞ the Father, Son and Holy Spirit orchestrated the divine plan that would protect His creation and remove all evil ∞ including satan.

Righteousness is produced by faith and its power is love. Abraham was counted righteous because of his faith, which is what pleases God. All faith has a corresponding action because it illustrates our trust in the invisible or spiritual world.

Because God is the substance of all things faith produces a visible result from trusting in the invisible Creator of all things.

That's why the prophetic has always been God's communication with man. Therefore, it's impossible to understand the Bible from a non-prophetic view. Prophetic timing is also critical because God doesn't live in time œ it lives in Him.

God used Abraham's faith to birth the nation of Israel. That bloodline was preserved and protected in order to redeem mankind, as well as condemn satan and his angels.

The immeasurable love of God compelled Him to restore man back to Himself. Therefore, before the foundation of the world He prepared the perfect plan of restoration that neither violated His righteousness or man's free will.

Man will never lose his right to choose, but all sin will be judged by **love, whose power is righteousness**. But what is righteousness?

The more I study the scriptures, the more I've determined righteousness is less about WHAT I do and more about WHY I do it. That really explains why God does what He does.

God is love. Righteousness is the power that makes love undefeatable.

I've heard people ask, "If there was a God of love why would He allow a tsunami or some other disaster?" People ask those difficult questions because they don't know that the responsibility of judgment is to protect love. Moreover, without judgment all life would be in chaos and eventually die.

Love both reproduces life and sustains it by judging anything that threatens it. **Righteousness demands darkness be judged to protect love from any corruption**.

Abraham's Righteousness

God defined the motives of Abraham as righteous because he believed. Those people who say they have faith should prove it with their actions. But even if their actions appear to be wrong their WHY for doing it can be correct according to God, because He judges the hearts of man.

The importance of acting from love defines Abraham's motives that believed God before he was circumcised. Circumcision was the identifying mark separating the Jews from the Gentiles, and an act of consecration to the Lord.

Therefore, before he was circumcised he was counted righteous. This means it's not what we do, but WHY we do it that receives the attention of God.

And he believed in the LORD, and He accounted it to him for righteousness.
Genesis 15:6

For in it the righteousness of God is revealed from faith to
faith; as it is written, "The just shall live by faith."
Romans 1:17

But he who doubts is condemned if he eats, because he
does not eat from faith; ***for whatever***
is not from faith is sin.
Romans 14:23

It's clear from the scriptures that unrighteousness or sin is produced from unbelief. Everyone is born with a "measure" of faith. That's God's divine connection with our spirit and it produces experiences that man identifies as intuition or *Déjà vu.*

The consciousness of this world is rooted in the fear of physical death because it hasn't been taught nor does it understand the spiritual realm. The world is ruled by the mindset of the unconverted mind of man which is filled with fear and selfishness.

Nothing is a surprise to God. Not the disobedience of Adam and not Lucifer's rebellion. God's majestic power and wisdom is beyond our comprehension. God is, after all, the Creator of everything and everyone. God found in Abraham a man who would establish His covenant and foreshadow His redemption. Abraham's faith changed the world and became the conduit for God's blessings.

Abraham was the bloodline God used to reproduce the *last Adam*. His seed of faith has multiplied into a blessing for all mankind.

In your seed all the nations of the earth shall be blessed, because you have obeyed My voice."
Genesis 22:18

Of this seed the Apostle Paul wrote:

*Now to Abraham and his **Seed** were the promises made. He does not say, "And to seeds," as of many, but as of one, "And to your **Seed**," who is Christ.*
Galatians 3:16

The importance of acting from love defines Abraham's motives that believed God and it was accounted as righteousness before he was circumcised. His action followed his faith, which is the natural order of things according to God. Why we act is predetermined by our faith or motives.

Isaac was the son God gave to Abraham for his faith. This was no ordinary birth. This was a miracle because his wife was barren. The greater test of his faith would come later when God asked Abraham to sacrifice Isaac. This was a foreshadowing of God's redemptive plan for mankind.

The blessing of Abraham is both physical and spiritual because of his obedience.

...that the blessing of Abraham might come upon the
Gentiles in Christ Jesus, that we might receive the promise
of the Spirit through faith.
Galatians 3:14

God made a promise to Abraham that became the cornerstone of the greatest plan ever created. It was through this father of faith that all those who would believe would be blessed.

Then the LORD appeared to Abram and said, "To your de-
scendants I will give this land." And there he built an altar
to the LORD, who had appeared to him.
Genesis 12:7

The LORD God of heaven, who took me from my father's
house and from the land of my family, and who spoke to me
and swore to me, saying, 'To your descendants I give this
land,' He will send His angel before you, and you shall
take a wife for my son from there.
Genesis 24:7

There are countless books written on the subject of faith and for very good reason because without faith we can't please God. But we must remember that faith is a spiritual force that produces both visible and invisible results.
Faith will produce a response from those who believe God. Faith isn't just for the purpose of receiving something from Him. It's a spiritual transaction that recognizes what He has already done.

God doesn't live in time and faith doesn't abide by our schedules. Faith is produced by God and given to man, in order for man to give it back to Him. The recognition of His faith produces an action born from thanksgiving, not need. One of the definitions of faith in Hebrews 11 describes faith as the *substance of things hoped for*. If we understand God as the Creator we must also acknowledge that nothing we want or hope for can have matter without Him.

In other words, attracting or manifesting the material of all things begins with recognizing Him as our Father. He rewards us by releasing His glory or righteousness into our beings, which is the invisible source of all things. This provokes us to want more of Him, not His creation.

But without faith it is impossible to please Him, for he who comes to God must believe that He is, and that He is a rewarder of those who diligently seek Him.
Hebrews 11:6

The riches of His glory are mentioned several times in the Epistles. My encounters with His glory began a spiritual transformation in me that altered my way of perceiving this dimension. It's the supernatural substance that empowers my faith. His riches are unlocking treasures too glorious to describe.

Jesus said, "*Anything is possible if you can believe.*" Do you want to change your physical condition? You can change it by your beliefs.

Jesus never said everything you desire is profitable for your spiritual development and produces the righteousness that pleases Him.

He said *you could have what you believe*. Therefore, without a converted soul our desires will be for more of His creation and not the Creator. The invisible realm responds to faith because God and faith are the same.

Solomon said, *"The blessing of the Lord makes one rich and adds no sorrow with it."* That means the blessing and riches are in knowing God as the source of all things. Sorrow will come to those who believe the material world is their source.

Believing God produces faith. Our beliefs originate from the heart and until our hearts are transformed by spiritual rebirth our unconverted mind will contaminate our desires, hopes and dreams.

Blessing of the First Son

Many know the story of Joseph, the son of Jacob who was sold into slavery in Egypt. After almost 22 years Jacob and Joseph were reunited. Before Jacob died he blessed his sons, including Joseph.

Now, something interesting happened as Jacob gave the blessing of the *first born* to his oldest son, Manasseh. During the ceremony God directed Jacob's hand to his youngest son, Ephraim. I believe this was to redeem what Cain stole from Abel.

The prophet Jeremiah reveals something significant which helps us understand the ways of God.

They departed in tears, but I will console them and guide them; I will lead them to brooks of water, on a level road, so that none shall stumble. For I am a father to Israel, Ephraim is my first-born.
Jeremiah 31:9 NAB

Isn't that interesting? God is choosing His first born who had nothing to do with Jacobs' son's natural order of birth.

God saw Ephraim as His first born. I know this may be obvious, but God doesn't think like man. We all say we know this, but when it comes to understanding the ways of God we use our reason to "figure" out His ways. This thinking leads to wrong decisions and flawed interpretations of the Bible.

Jacob also received the blessing of the first born from Esau and later Jacob contended for a blessing from God. He was given the name Israel at that time, which was the beginning of the blessing for Israel and the preparation of the "physical womb" to birth the Messiah.

The struggles and redemption of the Jewish people and even their participation in the crucifixion of Jesus was necessary to restore man back to God and condemn satan.

Throughout the Bible we are confounded by the way God determines righteousness.

This should awaken our spirit to the absolute necessity to depend on the Holy Spirit when it comes to making decisions or choices. His ways are higher than ours, but that's why He has given us His Spirit.

Prophets as a Faith Vortex

God uses prophets as a spiritual vortex for faith to change the material world. Abraham and his sons were prophets as identified by Jesus in the following scripture.

There will be weeping and gnashing of teeth, when you see Abraham and Isaac and Jacob and all the prophets in the kingdom of God, and yourselves thrust out.
Luke 13:28

Most people don't understand the absolute necessity of prophets. The power to believe what your senses can't detect is the door to God's kingdom. In fact, the Bible is clearly a prophetic book written cover-to-cover by the Spirit of Jesus.

Concerning this salvation, the prophets sought and searched diligently, who prophesied of the grace that would come to you:

searching for who or what kind of time the Spirit of Christ which was in them, pointed to, when he predicted the sufferings of Christ, and the glories that would follow them.
1 Peter 1:10, 11 WEB

> *And I fell at his feet to worship him. And he said to me,*
> *"Do not do that; I am a fellow servant of yours and your*
> *brethren who hold the testimony of Jesus; worship God.*
> **For the testimony of Jesus is the spirit of prophecy."**
> *Revelation 19:10 NASB*

As I said before, faith is a spiritual force that produces effects beyond our physical senses.

Those who spend time in worship and meditate on the kingdom of God will have experiences outside this physical dimension. The substance of faith is the power of righteousness that's seen in the invisible world.

I can remember on a number of occasions looking through what appeared to be a multicolored hole in the heavens. I saw many angelic-looking creatures. The most fascinating part of those visions was the feeling of peace and knowing that emanated from that portal or vortex.

These experiences have given me a greater understanding of the way Enoch just left this dimension and entered eternity. I believe one day the Lord will give me more insight into the dimensions outside of time and the opportunity to display it through worship.

Melchizedek, the high priest of heaven, was sent to bless Abraham, in order for the wealth of this world to be attracted, sent or transferred to those who are **born into the Son of God and Royal Priesthood.**

Christ Jesus by virtue of being from the seed of King David and after the order of Melchizedek is our Royal High Priest.

God responded to Abraham because of his faith. God made Abraham the father of many nations.

The wealth of the nations is the inheritance of those who are born into the Royal Priesthood. Christ Jesus is that Priest after the order of Melchizedek.

> ...where the forerunner has entered for us, even Jesus,
> having become High Priest forever
> according to the order of Melchizedek.
> Hebrews 6:20

But what does this mean and how does it affect you? Faith and righteousness opens the invisible realm to receive and distribute the riches from our Royal High Priest.

Abraham was shown our Messiah and rejoiced because he was chosen as the earthly seed for the spiritual heirs of Christ's kingdom.

> Your father Abraham rejoiced to see My day,
> and he saw it and was glad.
> John 8:56

God's perfect plan of restoration for all mankind began with Abraham and required a nation and bloodline to fulfill His ultimate strategy. The history of Israel played a critical role in fulfilling that perfect plan.

Moses was being prepared to take his position as the next part of God's perfect plan unfolds.

God told Abraham about the future of his offspring who became the nation of Israel.
He described their captivity and sufferings and even how long it would be before Moses delivered them.

Then He said to Abram: "Know certainly that your descendants will be strangers in a land that is not theirs, and will serve them, and they will afflict them four hundred years.
Genesis 15:13

The *last Adam*, Jesus, restored ALL that was lost. I emphasize "all" because most messages from the earliest reformers were about salvation through grace. God's Son, our Messiah restored ALL things lost by the first Adam.

Salvation is part of the restoration, but it's only a small part of the magnificent overcoming authority Christ obtained for those who are reborn into His image and likeness.

Abraham's faith provided the backdrop for the greatest drama ever to unfold on earth. His trust in God produced the offspring who formed the nation of Israel. Moreover, they were the conduits for both the Laws of God and the birth of God's *last Adam*. Jesus fulfilled every prophetic promise of the scriptures as a result of one man's faith.

The journey to reconcile man began with Abraham, who was counted righteous before the Laws of God. Nevertheless, Moses and the law were the next strategic step in God's exquisite plan.

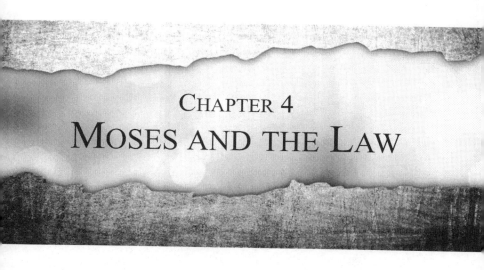

CHAPTER 4
MOSES AND THE LAW

God created all things including laws to govern the invisible and visible realms. Without laws angels and man couldn't be held accountable for their actions. God prepared hell for all created beings that choose darkness over light. However, because He is a righteous judge He couldn't execute judgment until His laws were violated. Murdering Jesus was the death sentence for satan and all who would follow after his ways.

God's laws are the visible masterpiece of God's invisible trap for satan. We learned that faith is the door to the heart of God, but sin forced mankind to listen and respond to fear.

God used signs and wonders to humble Egypt and frighten the Jews into submitting to His laws and Moses.

> *Then He said to Abram: "Know certainly that*
> *your descendants will be strangers in a land that is not*
> *theirs, and will serve them, and they will afflict*
> *them four hundred years. And also the nation whom they*
> *serve I will judge; afterward they shall come*
> *out with great possessions."*
> *Genesis 15:13, 14*

Moses was raised in Pharaoh's house and was being trained to lead Egypt. He might have become a Pharaoh had he not lost his temper and killed an Egyptian. I believe God's plan was for Moses to lead the people of God from royalty, not as a fugitive. I don't think the plagues and deaths of the Egyptians were God's first choice.

Remember, God told Abraham his descendants would be delivered after 400 years of captivity, but the scripture below reveals Moses didn't meet God's timetable.

> *Now the time that the sons of Israel lived in Egypt was*
> *four hundred and thirty years.*
> *Exodus 12:40 NASB*

Missing God's plan by thirty years may not sound like a big deal according to our way of thinking, but those who understand the preciseness of God know that timing is everything!

The Element of Timing

Timing determines position that affects our correct understanding at so many levels. For example, have you ever read a book that was missing the last chapter?
Or have you listened to instructions on the phone when a plane flies overhead? You are left to fill in the blanks by your best guess or speculations.

God uses time, but He isn't restricted by it because He resides in eternity. Man has only a limited amount of time to understand the ways of God. That's why Moses wanted to know His ways. When God speaks His Word is fulfilled outside of time, but His voice is received in each generation according to our level of knowledge about Him. We physically occupy three dimensions, but His desires and will are multidimensional. In fact, His desires have already been completed in eternity or before the foundation of time.

The plans of God will prevail, but our participation or lack of participation will be according to our sensitivity to His Spirit. His mercy and grace supersedes wrath and judgment to those whose hearts are turned toward Him.

In other words, God will have His way, but we can miss great blessings or impartations that may have prepared us for a future event or provided tools that make completing our current task easier.

For example, had Moses not been a fugitive he wouldn't have married a Midianite. We'll discover later that this led to him governing from a system that was from man, not God.

Moses had the largest congregation ever to assemble under the name of God. They witnessed the greatest miracles ever recorded. In spite of this, of the first generation all but Joshua and Caleb died without entering the Promised Land. I believe the congregation wandering in the wilderness then is a picture of the church today.

Christ completed everything for mankind at the cross. But our failure to understand the totality of that event has led to fundamentally missing the ways of God. We will then reason that what He used in the Old Testament is what we need now. But we have a New Covenant with greater rewards and blessings for those who diligently seek Him by His Spirit.

God is the God of the living, not the dead. That means what He did yesterday was marvelous, but if you aren't paying attention to His ways now you will miss the glorious blessings He has for your life today. People are eager to be part of large congregations whose leaders are charismatic and operate in miracles. The structures of today's churches are designed to make people comfortable and control them much like the laws given to Moses.

Man's Idea or God's Idea?

For example, was it a God idea or a good idea to divide the multitude up with judges for thousands, hundreds, fifties and tens? This idea came from Moses' father-in-law, Jethro who was a Midianite. These people worshiped idols and were continually fighting against the Israelites.

Listen now to my voice; I will give you counsel, and God will be with you: Stand before God for the people, so that you may bring the difficulties to God.

Moreover you shall select from all the people able men, such as fear God, men of truth, hating covetousness; and place such over them to be rulers of thousands, rulers of hundreds, rulers of fifties, and rulers of tens.

And let them judge the people at all times. Then it will be that every great matter they shall bring to you, but every small matter they themselves shall judge. So it will be easier for you, for they will bear the burden with you.

If you do this thing, and God so commands you, then you will be able to endure, and all this people will also go to their place in peace.

So Moses heeded the voice of his father-in-law and did all that he had said.
Exodus 18:19, 21-24

I always wondered why Moses, who heard God, would listen to someone who never heard from God. Then the Lord reminded me of my own eagerness over the years to hear from others instead of from Him. This is a weakness inside men who secretly want someone to blame if things don't go as planned. I've repented from that structure in my life. I now listen to the Holy Spirit for myself and take the responsibility for what I hear.

God is raising a new breed of leaders who will embrace problems with God-kind of solutions without fear of reprisal from men. Over the years I've learned the more attention I pay to the Spirit, the greater the chances for me to receive solutions that change hearts not just circumstances.

Notice that Jethro tells Moses "God **may be with you**." This is after he tells Moses something very revealing.

> *Now he had said to Moses, "I, your father-in-law*
> *Jethro, am coming to you with your wife and*
> *her two sons with her."*
> *Exodus 18:6*

I believe Jethro never liked the Jews and as a priest for the Midianites he was separating his family from Moses. Even though God included them and had the boys circumcised, Jethro's heart served the idols he worshipped.

Therefore, although the advice sounded good and supplied a structure to the circumstances it wasn't the counsel of God. History proved that these people often and violently turned on Moses after he instituted this process – proving it wasn't from God. The same thing was true when the Israelites chose Saul as king instead of following God through the prophet Samuel.

Consequently, the structures of many churches today are formed from this mindset. This governmental system produces a culture of division and rebellion. It's founded not from the voice of God or prophets, but from guidelines and principals of those who use reason and are not led by the Spirit.

So I will call you Peter, which means "a rock."
On this rock I will build my church, and death itself
will not have any power over it.
Matthew 16:18 CEV

Jesus tells Peter after he identifies Jesus as "the Christ" that His Church will be built upon an ever ascending revelation of the Christ. He uses the word "rock" to represent both the visible and invisible realm. The foundation for God's Church will be built upon revelation, not man's reasoning or good ideas.

The wrong foundation will never produce the desired result from God regardless of the way it looks or sounds. We must constantly challenge what and why we believe the way we do.

Otherwise, a wrong foundation will be built and it will offer little resistance to the trials of this life.

Bible scholars who have counted the laws and commandments given to Moses find there are over 600. The Ten Commandments aren't even counted among them. Is it any wonder the Israelites were so legalistic during the time of Christ?

Legalism is one of the problems facing today's church. The Holy Spirit will use any opportunity He has to introduce people to Christ. Many times people experience Him in religious settings that don't necessarily reflect the "ways" of God.

When the new Believer doesn't understand the ways of God he associates the experience with the method. They quickly adapt concepts that form structures without substance most commonly referred to as religion.

But Christ destroyed the yoke of religion and opened the door to His kingdom for those willing to trust His Spirit. Righteous living for Christ Jesus requires a radical shift in your believing and current knowledge of Him. All experiences you have ever had with Him are designed to provoke you to pursue Him. If leaders would train the people to hear the Holy Spirit their influence would increase in their cities and nations, without having to rely on models from this world.

Moses' Role

Moses' role in God's majestic plan to redeem mankind and condemn satan could only have been orchestrated by our

Heavenly Father. The results are ever unfolding to those who have eyes and ears for His Spirit.

Remember, God made a promise to Abraham. It was because of Abraham's faith that he would be the father of many nations. If faith was always the key back to God why did He institute the law?

The Apostle Paul, more than anyone, understood the transition from Abraham to Moses to Christ. Perhaps, he was able to explain it so well because of his transformation from Saul to Paul.

The purpose of the law was to keep a sinful people in the way of salvation until Christ (the descendant) came, *inheriting the promises and distributing them to us. Obviously this law was not a firsthand encounter with God. It was arranged by angelic messengers through a middleman, Moses.*

But if there is a middleman as there was at Sinai, then the people are not dealing directly with God, are they? But the original promise is the direct blessing of God, received by faith.

If such is the case, is the law, then, an anti-promise, a negation of God's will for us? Not at all. ***Its purpose was to make obvious to everyone that we are, in ourselves, out of right relationship with God,*** *and therefore to show us the futility of devising some religious system for getting by our own efforts what we can only get by waiting in faith*

for God to complete his promise. For if any kind of rule-keeping had power to create life in us, we would certainly have gotten it by this time.
Galatians 3:19-21 Message

We were kept under control by Moses' laws until this faith came. *We were under their control until this faith which was about to come would be revealed.*

Before Christ came, Moses' laws served as our guardian. *Christ came so that we could receive God's approval by faith.* **But now that this faith has come, we are no longer under the control of a guardian.**
Galatians 3:23-25 GWT

God doesn't accept people simply because they obey the Law. No, indeed! **All the Law does is to point out our sin.**

Now we see how God does make us acceptable to him. **The Law and the Prophets tell how we become acceptable, and it isn't by obeying the Law of Moses.**

God treats everyone alike. **He accepts people only because they have faith in Jesus Christ.**

All of us have sinned and fallen short of God's glory.
Romans 3:20-23 CEV

These scriptures explain one of the purposes of the law was to expose man to his transgression against God.

The hidden reason that wasn't obvious was to trap satan within his own system of laws. This was the secret of the ages and part of the manifold wisdom of Christ.

Satan's System of Wisdom

Man chose satan's system of wisdom when he ate from the tree of the knowledge of good and evil. That's the current world system we are born into because of the choice of the first Adam. Mankind couldn't keep the laws of right and wrong because only God is capable of that. Therefore, satan had legal right to judge mankind for his lawlessness.

This authority was clearly displayed in the Book of Job, which is considered by most theologians to be the oldest book in the Bible.

One day when the sons of God came to stand in front of the Lord, Satan the Accuser came along with them.

*The Lord asked Satan, "Where have you come from?"
Satan answered the Lord, "From wandering
all over the earth."
Job 1:6, 7*

*The Lord told Satan, "He is in your power,
but you must spare his life!"*

*Satan left the Lord's presence and struck Job with painful
boils from the soles of his feet to the top of his head.
Job 2:6, 7*

The material world, including man, operates according to universal laws. The rules governing man were enforced by satan until Christ redeemed us from lawlessness. God's commandments are universal and must be kept by all beings œ including satan and his angels. The laws given to Moses were the two-edged sword from God that redeemed Israel and dammed satan.

Salvation First for the Jews

But Israel is saved by the LORD with everlasting
salvation; you shall not be put to shame or
confounded to all eternity.
Isaiah 45:17 ESV

Jesus said to him, "Today, salvation has come to this
house, because he also is a son of Abraham.
Luke 19:9

You worship what you do not know; we know what
we worship, for salvation is of the Jews.
John 4:22

The law provided a bonus to the household of Israel: salvation. God showed the whole world that following His laws returned a portion of what the first Adam lost in the beginning. They were abundantly blessed in material wealth including victories over their enemies. Israel's blessings became their downfall because they forgot God's laws were spiritual and therefore required faith.

God used the faith of Abraham to unfold His majestic plan that included the birth of the nation Israel. Salvation was the first part of God's reconciliation for mankind and Moses was His instrument.

The true descendants of God are birthed by faith the same as those from Abraham. For example, Jacob became Israel after wrestling with the angel from the Lord. Saul became Paul after his experience on the road to Damascus. These are examples of men who received salvation by keeping the law, but a further transformation was necessary to fulfill their highest callings.

Many of you are being prepared for marvelous adventures. Some of them will be even greater than you can think or imagine, but a greater transformation is needed in your lives. Now is your time to search out the new birth Jesus explains to Nicodemus in John 3.

The Bible says the law came through Moses, but grace and truth by Jesus Christ. We are going to look at grace in a different way.

CHAPTER 5
GOSPEL OF GRACE

One day I was walking to church and noticed a homeless man with a tin cup asking for money sitting outside the church. I remember being angry that he would dare to disrespect "God's house" in that way. As I approached him my heart beat faster with the anticipation of telling him just how I felt. Before I could open my mouth, a big man with broad shoulders rushed by me with $20. He put it in the tin cup and said, "Jesus loves you" and walked away. I stopped and thought about that for a minute. I knew Jesus loved me, but I thought that was because I "tried" to be good and follow what my pastor taught me about the Bible.

It's taken me years to discover that what I do is less important to Christ than why I do it. The message of grace is not a new religion, but it's the unveiling of Christ in His resurrected glory. Grace opens a wide door into His mysteries that begins with our salvation, but it doesn't end there. The further you go into "Truth" the more narrow the opening gets until the person you were can no longer continue. Then at a certain point you must make a decision to lose your identity and mindset and submit to the King of Kings.

We have entered a season that's unveiling more revelation of the Person of Grace. This has exposed us to greater responsibilities. I'm not talking about earning our salvation with works or efforts. I'm referring to the response you make after recognizing the magnitude of such love.

For example, how would you react if someone gave you a million dollars out of love? In a sense, that's exactly what Christ did for you. Once we understand what we have freely been given our lives must reflect a gratitude that's beyond the concept of "earning" our salvation.

Grace is not free. It cost God His Son. How you react to that love defines your faith.

Do we then make void the law through faith? Certainly not! On the contrary, we establish the law.
Romans 3:31

Therefore it is of faith that it might be according to grace, so that the promise might be sure to all the seed, not only to those who are of the law, but also to those who are of the faith of Abraham, who is the father of us all.
Romans 4:16

"I do not set aside the grace of God; for if righteousness comes through the law, then Christ died in vain."
Galatians 2:21

Moreover the law entered that the offense might abound. But where sin abounded, grace abounded much more,
Romans 5:20

For sin shall not have dominion over you, for you are not under law but under grace.
Romans 6:14

The law was critical in the majestic plan of God. It not only began the reconciliation of mankind and returned God's kingdom to His sons, but it just as importantly condemned satan. This was only achieved through God's grace, which is the very Person of Christ Jesus.

For the Law was given through Moses, but grace and truth came through Jesus Christ.
John 1:17

I remind you that everything we discuss in this *Ever Ascending: The Resurrection Series* will be from the spiritual perspective.

For example, the verse that describes the "law" coming "through" Moses. Moses was the vessel God used to deliver His law, but Moses spent 40 days twice in the presence of God without food or water. No human being could survive that long without water. That encounter changed both his outward countenance and inner man. In my opinion, Moses was the spiritual manifestation of God's laws. Moreover, Jesus is the expressed image of God and as such represents Him as both the grace and truth.

The revelation of Him as God's grace is the most powerful piece in God's majestic plan to reconcile mankind and return what the first Adam lost.

> *For we know that **the law is spiritual**,*
> *but I am carnal, sold under sin.*
> *Romans 7:14*

Most people have heard the definition of grace as "unmerited favor." **Obviously, that describes the word, but not the Person of Christ or His work**. The power and work of grace isn't in defining the word, but in understanding its power.

The spiritual fact is Moses was the Law of God in the flesh just as Jesus is the Grace and Truth. The reality of that verse can't be understood without an encounter with the Person of Christ who is Grace. Grace is the door to Truth, which is the Person of Christ who is unveiled to those "born" of His Spirit.

Man often uses the word grace to describe a financial courtesy extended to those who need extra time to pay their debts, loans or insurance policies. **God, however, uses grace to destroy the works of the devil and to restore what the first Adam lost.** Grace is perhaps the greatest expression of God's love ever to be released.

The completed work of Christ can take an eternity to understand. That's why it's veiled in religion and misunderstood by those who interpret the scriptures without the Holy Spirit. The mystery and power of Christ to me is captured in the title of this series Ever Ascending.

One day while meditating on some passages I looked up and saw what appeared to be golden lines and circles moving in several directions at once. They would intersect with each other and change figures and form patterns that were both familiar and unfamiliar to me. At one point it became apparent that these shapes moved outside of the 3rd dimension. Suddenly, the form that was familiar transformed into something totally different because it moved into another dimension.

The Holy Spirit immediately said that the Bible is a spiritual book with the power to transform anyone at any level or dimension. This is the multidimensional or *ever ascending* power in the resurrection of Christ.

That encounter has shattered my preconceived ideas and images of Christ.

I've recognized the absolute necessity to receive fresh revelation each day in order to expand my knowledge and sensitivity to His completed work. The more I learn, the more apparent it is that the *last Adam* has established God's kingdom.

Those who make the effort to break with tradition and listen to His voice will hear a new sound of victory and authority that will stir up their passion and anger towards sin. This sound will empower you to rip the veil of religion and enter into the spiritual realm where God's kingdom **reigns**.

> *Whoever has been born of God does not sin,*
> *for His seed remains in him; and he cannot sin,*
> *because he has been born of God.*
> *1 John 3:9*

Paul was the expert on grace and its connection with salvation. In fact, he was anointed and assigned to preach the grace message.

> *But none of these things move me; nor do I count my life*
> *dear to myself, so that I may finish my race with joy, and*
> *the ministry which I received from the Lord Jesus, to testify*
> *to the gospel of the grace of God.*
> *Acts 20:24*

During my early years as a Believer I studied Paul's Epistles especially Romans 10:9, 10.

*That if thou shalt confess with thy mouth the Lord Jesus,
and shalt believe in thine heart that God hath raised him
from the dead, thou shalt be **saved**.*

*For with the heart man believeth unto righteousness; and
with the mouth confession is made unto **salvation**.*
Romans 10:9, 10

*For by grace you have been saved through faith, and that
not of yourselves; it is the gift of God,*
Ephesians 2:8

*...even when we were dead in trespasses, made us alive
together with Christ (by grace you have been saved),*
Ephesians 2:5

*...desires all men to be saved and to come to the
knowledge of the truth.*
1 Timothy 2:4

Paul had the greatest revelation of grace - perhaps more than
all the other disciples. He was a Pharisee of Pharisees, which
gave him powerful insight into both the mind of the Jew and
the heart of God.

Most Believers are familiar with the Law of Moses. And
many identify Jesus as God's only begotten Son who
sacrificed His life on a cross so we can go to heaven. This is
the message commonly called the "gospel of salvation"
among the Evangelicals, Charismatics and Protestants.

The word gospel also means "good news." There's no greater news than Jesus, the Son of God sacrificing His life so we may live eternally with Him.

After reading the first four chapters you should be acquainted with the devastation and consequences of sin. There's no way to describe the utter despair and terror of living in torment for eternity. Imagine the agony of only feeling pain, smelling sulfur, hearing bloodcurdling screams and seeing darkness for eternity.

Moreover, our soul will replay our decision to reject Christ or His word for all eternity. It's a hollow, empty, lost feeling of knowing you made the choice and there is nothing you or God can do about it.

So many people believe the wrong things because they listen to wicked voices. Before long the damage to their soul is so widespread that aside from a miracle it's impossible for them to believe anything other than what their senses discern. That's the consciousness of this world that was born from the original deception of sin in the Garden of Eden.

Nevertheless, we don't know what happens to people in their last seconds before death. That's the glory of salvation and why Jesus paid the ultimate price. He wanted to assure God, our Heavenly Father, that mankind has a choice œ even in the final nanosecond of their life.

And it shall come to pass that whoever calls on the name of the LORD Shall be saved.
Joel 2:32a

Salvation was for the Jewish people who kept the law until Christ completed His work. That work included reestablishing God's kingdom on earth. Jesus is the "grace" of God in physical form. The Gospel of Salvation still requires faith and is possible because of God's grace. Jesus is the prophetic laws of God and as His Grace and He removed all transgression.

The gospel of salvation is "the" message Paul preached and it's available to all who call upon our Lord Jesus. Nevertheless, it's only the introduction of His completed work which is ever unfolding in the message of God's kingdom.

CHAPTER 6
THE MANY GOSPELS

The Bible is the "good news" or gospel for all mankind, but until Jesus was born the word gospel wasn't used in the scriptures. The gospel I heard preached in churches was that of salvation because it was from the Epistles that Paul wrote. Paul had such an encounter with God's grace, in the Person of Christ that he was given the assignment to preach that gospel. Moreover, Paul was a scholar of the Jewish law and with the help of the Holy Spirit he was able to see Christ as both the Messiah and the Grace of God.

Believers today are often confused because all of the messages they hear portrayed as the "gospel" seem to be the same.

The truth is that most of them, however, are the *gospel of salvation* that was preached by the Apostle Paul.

Until sin, however, there was only one gospel between man and God. The "good news" was that earth was joined with the heavens and there was no death, sickness, disease or evil. Sin destroyed the connection between the Creator and His creation and forced God to crucify His only Son to save all those who would believe in Jesus. That concept of the gospel has become today's gospel or "good news."

Generally speaking, that's one aspect of what Jesus did, but it shouldn't be confused with the message He Himself preached. His message is and was the spiritual transforming message of the kingdom that requires a spiritual rebirth. Jesus describes this process to Nicodemus in John 3. We will discuss this spiritual rebirth in greater detail in the following chapter.

Our faith is the spiritual power that releases God's grace. Each "gospel" imparts the faith of the person presenting it and represents that person's revelation of Christ. God sent His gospel through Jesus Christ who is Grace and Truth. Those presenting "the gospel" should understand this, as well as those who profess to believe "the gospel."

The Covenants

Before describing the various gospels it's important to understand His commitment to man was established originally by covenant. This is the building block for Christ and His kingdom.

God would never allow His creation to be destroyed or stolen because of man's weakness.

God began His redemption plan and covenant with His first son, Adam by killing animals or shedding blood to clothe Adam and Eve.

Also for Adam and his wife the LORD God made
tunics of skin, and clothed them.
Genesis 3:21

The same method was used by satan to rule over man. Satan used Abel's blood to seal his covenant with mankind. This introduced sin as a spiritual virus into our DNA.

Now Cain talked with Abel his brother; and it came to pass, when they were in the field, that Cain rose up against Abel his brother and killed him.

And He said, "What have you done? The voice of your
brother's blood cries out to Me from the ground."
Genesis 4:8, 10

Throughout the Old Testament God made covenants with men such as Noah, Abraham, Isaac, Jacob, Moses and David. There were others, but these are the key figures God used to complete His majestic plan through Christ.

Moses built an Ark that contained the prophetic covenant God made with the Jews. This was a type of salvation before The Messiah. All covenants were established between God and man for man's salvation. All of these "Old Testament" covenants were gospels or "good news" for the generations of that time.

Salvation and Gospel

It wasn't until after Jesus was born that the term "gospel" began to be used. That's why it's so easy to see the connection between the word gospel and salvation. This is a critical concept to understand because it's most likely responsible for so much confusion between salvation and the "new birth."

The author of Hebrews speaks about "the gospel" during the time of Moses in the wilderness.

For indeed the gospel was preached to us as well as to them; but the word, which they heard did not profit them, not being mixed with faith in those who heard it.
Hebrews 4:2

This scripture refers to the people wandering in the wilderness with Moses.

The writer, which many scholars believe is Paul, is talking about the **gospel of salvation**. That generation witnessed the greatest display of God's miracles — more than anyone else ever to live. The supernatural was commonplace. They woke up daily to have "fresh bread" delivered from heaven above. So, they lived in the supernatural beginning with their bread and water to having a front row seat observing God's Shekinah glory.

They didn't need faith to observe with their physical senses what happened right before their eyes. The law, however, is spiritual and requires faith to believe so consequently they didn't qualify to enter God's promises.

The law was God's covenant that saved His chosen people, Israel who provided the bloodline and prophetic word that manifested the Messiah.
Unfortunately, the law blinded them to the glorious gospel in the Person of Christ Jesus.

*...whose minds the god of this age has blinded, who do not believe, **lest the light of the gospel of the glory of Christ**, who is the image of God, should shine on them.*
2 Corinthians 4:4

Gospel of Paul

Paul was literally transformed from Saul to Paul after his experience with Christ on the road to Damascus. After that encounter, Paul understood his purpose and call.

This is the kind of encounter that Jesus describes to Nicodemus as the "rebirth" which is critical for all of us to fulfill our destinies.

As he journeyed he came near Damascus, and suddenly a light shone around him from heaven. Then he fell to the ground, and heard a voice saying to him, "Saul, Saul, why are you persecuting Me?"

And he said, "Who are You, Lord?"

Then the Lord said, "I am Jesus, whom you are persecuting. It is hard for you to kick against the goads."

So he, trembling and astonished, said,
"Lord, what do You want me to do?"
Then the Lord said to him, "Arise and go into the city, and you will be told what you must do."
Acts 9:3-6

The Bible says Paul was blind and he neither ate nor drank for three days. He was exposed to extraordinary revelation during that time. We can learn something about fasting from Paul's experience. The first steps in discovering the spiritual realm is to eliminate our senses from the decision making process of our lives. Perhaps, that's why I'm such a proponent of fasting. Fasting has been a key to opening my eyes to both wisdom and to many things of the kingdom hidden in plain sight.

The following scriptures describe the specific message that Paul preached.

But none of these things move me; nor do I count my life dear to myself, so that I may finish my race with joy, and the ministry which I received from the Lord Jesus, to testify to the gospel of the grace of God.
Acts 20:24

Paul, a bondservant of Jesus Christ, called to be an apostle, separated to the gospel of God...
Romans 1:1

*...in the day when God will judge the secrets of men by Jesus Christ, according to **my gospel**.*
Romans 2:16

*Now to Him who is able to establish you **according to my gospel** and the preaching of Jesus Christ, according to the revelation of the mystery kept secret since the world began.*
Romans 16:25

*Remember Jesus Christ, arisen from the dead, descendant of David, according to **my gospel**...*
2 Timothy 2:8

For I am not ashamed of the gospel of Christ, for it is the power of God to salvation for everyone who believes, for the Jew first and also for the Greek.
Romans 1:16

*Paul, a bondservant of Jesus Christ, called to be an
apostle, separated to the **gospel of God**...*
Romans 1:1

*...in mighty signs and wonders, by the power of the Spirit
of God, so that from Jerusalem and round about to
Illyricum I have fully preached the gospel of Christ.*
Romans 15:19

*...and having shod your feet with the preparation
of the **gospel of peace**;*
Ephesians 6:15

In these scriptures we find that Paul was given an assignment
to preach a "gospel" that produced salvation to all who
believed. That gospel is NOT the same as the **gospel of the
kingdom** preached by Christ. All "the gospels" require faith
to activate that particular revelation of Christ. Moreover,
they all contain the power of salvation.

*And when there had been much dispute, Peter rose up and
said to them: "Men and brethren, you know that a good
while ago God chose among us, that by my mouth the Gentiles should hear the word of the gospel and believe.*
Acts 15:7

**Each of the disciples preached a gospel that was specific
to their revelation of Jesus. But Jesus was the only one
who could preach the Kingdom of God because that is
who He is. One can only preach the message that they
carry or that is alive inside them.**

Gospel of the Kingdom

Daniel and Matthew refer to the kingdom of God more than any other books in the Bible. Daniel was prophesying the return of what the first Adam lost and His eternal reign on earth as it is in heaven.

> *Then the kingdom and dominion, and the greatness*
> *of the kingdoms under the whole heaven, shall be given to*
> *the people, the saints of the Most High. His kingdom*
> *is an everlasting kingdom, and all dominions shall*
> *serve and obey Him.*
> *Daniel 7:27*

The Jews understood the history of kingdoms, but they were expecting a physical manifestation of God's power ending with the Messiah sitting on the throne of David in Jerusalem.

> *Now when He was asked by the Pharisees when the*
> *kingdom of God would come, He answered them and said,*
> ***"The kingdom of God does not come with observation…"***
> *Luke 17:20*

This was the major stumbling block for the Jewish leaders because they wanted a sign in order to believe. The signs their fathers saw in Egypt and the desert trained them to believe what they could see. That mentality has been passed down throughout all religions. Most people only want to believe what their senses can perceive.

John the Baptist was the person God used to prepare the way for Jesus and to announce the arrival of the kingdom.

In those days John the Baptist came preaching in the wilderness of Judea, and saying, "Repent, for the kingdom of heaven is at hand!"
Matthew 3:1, 2

*From that time began Jesus to preach and to say, "Repent; for **the kingdom of heaven** is at hand."*
Matthew 4:17

*And Jesus went about in all Galilee, teaching in their synagogues, preaching the **gospel of the kingdom**, and healing all kinds*
of sickness and all kinds of disease among the people.
Matthew 4:23

*But seek first the **kingdom of God** and His righteousness, and all these things shall be added to you.*
Matthew 6:33

*Then Jesus went about all the cities and villages, teaching in their synagogues, **preaching the gospel of the kingdom**, and healing every sickness and every disease among the people.*
Matthew 9:35

Notice that signs and wonders followed the message of Jesus. The message Paul and the other disciples preached also produced signs and wonders, but it was because of their faith in the Person of Christ. This is the most important point to emphasize.

The kingdom message Jesus delivered was as the last Adam. That gospel is different from all the other gospels because Jesus was exposing the Christ as the kingdom and God validated it through His resurrection.

> *For the law was given through Moses,*
> *but grace and **truth came through Jesus Christ.***
> *John 1:17*

God's kingdom and His righteousness is Christ and it must be the most important desire for anyone who wants to know "the" Truth. Jesus is the kingdom and those who enter Him in the new birth will be a living gospel of His kingdom.

Those birthed into Christ are equipped to preach the message of the kingdom. That's the glorious gospel which reveals Christ and introduces us to the Holy Spirit as our covering. But it's not some organization or denomination. It's the manifested presence and dominion of the living Christ on earth and in heaven the same way it was with the first Adam.

The gospel of salvation isn't the same gospel Jesus preached. The most profound truth I've discovered in the scriptures is that everyone who receives a revelation of Christ is given their own personal gospel to preach.

It will transform both the speaker and the listener as they allow His revelation to ever ascend.

But don't be confused. There's only ONE KINGDOM GOSPEL and that's Christ. His kingdom is the transforming, invisible power over all powers and principalities visible and invisible. Those who minister that kingdom must be positioned inside Him through a new birth.

CHAPTER 7
THE LAST ADAM

The *last Adam* has reinstated on earth what was lost. The majestic plan of God has abolished the slavery and tyranny of satan over mankind. Salvation alone is not sufficient to understand what the *last Adam* has accomplished. That understanding requires being reborn by His Water and Spirit.

The power to see the invisible kingdom of God isn't achieved with our unconverted mindset. The word repent isn't just the choice to stop certain behaviors.

But it's the authority that you receive because you made the choice to change the way you think. No one can enter God's kingdom without a spiritual rebirth that strips you of your identity to this world.

And so it is written, "The first man Adam became a living being." The last Adam became a life-giving spirit.
1 Corinthians 15:45

We've arrived at what may be the most powerful and yet least understood part in God's grand design. There can be no mistake about the purpose of Jesus and His transformation into Christ at His resurrection. The quintessential power to rule and reign alongside Christ for eternity is determined by our desire to enter His kingdom now.

Jesus, the Son of man, had a specific assignment to complete the perfect plan He and His Father designed before the foundation of the world. This included the very people they would use to fulfill the job.

...although the works were finished from the foundation of the world.
Hebrews 4:3b

But He answered and said, "I was not sent except to the lost sheep of the house of Israel."
Matthew 15:24

Jesus was specifically sent to the Jews. This didn't prevent others from getting healed or delivered, but His assignment was to the Jews. They were the people God chose because He is God, not because they were special.

It is not because of your righteousness or the uprightness of your heart that you go in to possess their land, but because of the wickedness of these nations that the LORD your God drives them out from before you, and that He may fulfill the word which the LORD swore to your fathers, to Abraham, Isaac, and Jacob.

Therefore understand that the LORD your God is not giving you this good land to possess because of your righteousness, for you are a stiff-necked people.
Deuteronomy 9:5, 6

The Law of Moses served its purpose, but God wanted all mankind not just Israel. Remember, all humanity was corrupted by sin through Adam's bloodline. Therefore, the last Adam would fulfill His part as the spotless Lamb of God by carrying His Father's blood.

This is He who came by water and blood — Jesus Christ; not only by water, but by water and blood. And it is the Spirit who bears witness, because the Spirit is truth.
1 John 5:6

The importance of that verse will become clear as you read about the new birth described to Nicodemus.

Jesus couldn't have destroyed the work of satan and remove him from rulership without the Father's blood.

He who sins is of the devil, for the devil has sinned from the beginning. For this purpose the Son of God was manifested, that He might destroy the works of the devil.
1 John 3:8

Every Old Testament prophet spoke of the Messiah and the restoration of "the kingdom," but they didn't understand it was to include the whole world and not just Israel. That's a problem today, especially with most messages, that use the words "gospel" or "kingdom." Unfortunately, many people have a limited understanding of the spiritual realm or the difference between the message Jesus delivered and the gospel of salvation.

The Last Adam's Transformation

Understanding and entering the full work of the *last Adam* doesn't happen overnight or with an altar call. It's a process that only the Holy Spirit initiates and completes.

 strongest resistance to trusting the Holy Spirit always comes from our minds and consciousness. The mind fights to regain control and authority by challenging everything it can't verify through the five senses.

Transforming our mindset isn't easy, but the message of the kingdom Jesus preached provides the only solution for that, and it's called "born again."

There was a man of the Pharisees named Nicodemus, a ruler of the Jews. This man came to Jesus by night and said to Him, "Rabbi, we know that You are a teacher come from God; for no one can do these signs that You do unless God is with him."

*Jesus answered and said to him, "Most assuredly, I say to you, unless one is **born again, he cannot see the kingdom of God**."Nicodemus said to Him, "How can a man be born when he is old? Can he enter a second time into his mother's womb and be born?"*

*Jesus answered, "Most assuredly, I say to you, **unless one is born of water and the Spirit, he cannot enter the kingdom of God**. That which is born of the flesh is flesh, and that which is born of the Spirit is spirit.*
John 3:1-6

First and foremost, don't confuse the Gospel of Salvation with the Gospel of the Kingdom. THEY ARE NOT THE SAME. One can be saved but never enter into God's Kingdom.

Nowhere in the conversation with Nicodemus does Jesus speak about salvation. He most certainly describes the transformation that occurs when you are "born again."

Every birth requires a womb. Jesus had to be born of a woman in the natural to fulfill His purpose and assignment on the earth. His physical death and resurrection produced the spiritual womb for us to be born into His kingdom.

This makes no sense in the natural and only adds to the confusion of those trying to understand the scriptures.

There's a scripture that can help you see the reality and depth of being reborn, while still in your physical bodies. Study the description of Jesus on the Mount of Transfiguration. In my opinion, Jesus is visibly displaying the image of the first Adam and those who would be "born again."

And He said to them, "Assuredly, I say to you that there are some standing here who will not taste death till they see the kingdom of God present with power."

Now after six days Jesus took Peter, James, and John, and led them up on a high mountain apart by themselves; and He was transfigured before them. His clothes became shining, exceedingly white, like snow, such as no launderer on earth can whiten them. And Elijah appeared to them with Moses, and they were talking with Jesus.
Mark 9:1-4

The transformation of Jesus revealed He was the kingdom of God and the door into the invisible realm of eternal life. Moreover, His death and resurrection was about to forever destroy the hold death had over mankind because of sin. The *last Adam* was returning all that was lost by the first Adam.

The experience described by Jesus as the "new birth" rips the veil between the spiritual and material worlds.

This "new birth" reveals the majestic kingdom of God outside the dimensions of time and space that was established before the foundation of the world.

The consciousness of sin in this dimension has blinded our ability to understand the *ever ascending* power available to those who do whatever it takes to enter His kingdom. Christ paid the ultimate price not only for our salvation, but also for our eternal abiding in Him now. This isn't a future event. It begins the instant you repent and recognize Christ as having fulfilled His assignment. He reestablished what the first Adam lost namely God's Kingdom.

There are countless stories of men and women of God who have experienced miraculous events. Every story describes things beyond our five senses. Some have told of being translated instantly to distant places; or walking invisibly through prison walls; or being rescued by angels; or speaking with apostles of old, and on and on.

I'm reminded of a story about John G. Lake that describes him being translated to South Africa to battle œ in the spiritual realm œ a demonic legion attacking people with epilepsy and mental illness. He speaks about the Lord taking him to a high mountain to command angels in that region to fight these evil spirits. He said the people in South Africa at that time didn't understand spiritual warfare. Therefore, the Lord transported his spirit thousands of miles to command the host of angels to do the battle.

God is no respecter of persons. What he has done for one; He can do for all. We need to get a revelation that heaven is now and the only thing preventing us from living in the supernatural is our unconverted mind. The transformation from the mindset of the first Adam to the last Adam begins in His Water and Spirit.

Characteristics of the Last Adam

A. Jesus, the Kingdom

...and saying, "The time is fulfilled, and the kingdom of God is at hand. Repent, and believe in the gospel."
Mark 1:15

We previously explained the difference between the gospel of salvation and the message of the kingdom Jesus preached. I want to emphasize this through the verse in Mark 1 where Jesus is the gospel of the kingdom. When He says, "repent and believe in the gospel" He is speaking about changing your mindset and perception in order to enter into Him.

Believing in "a gospel" doesn't change your mindset. It just offers another system to follow. This is precisely what happens to most people today who say they believe in Jesus. Very little happens or changes in their lives because their minds aren't altered. The fact is that they may have had an emotional experience, but that will pass and so too will their commitment to Christ.

This doesn't mean they aren't saved nor will the Holy Spirit abandon them. On the contrary, God uses every means possible to draw them into deeper and deeper experiences with His Holy Spirit.

The gospel of the kingdom isn't like any other message because it produces not only signs and wonders, but also a transformation in your mindset. It demands a violent restructuring of our mental faculties. That's what the word repent means.

> *And from the days of John the Baptist until now*
> *the kingdom of heaven suffers violence, and the*
> *violent take it by force.*
> *Matthew 11:12*

The opposition to the real message of the kingdom is unnatural and spiritual because those who hear it and believe it are transformed in their spirit, soul and body.

B. Jesus, the Substance of All Things

Anyone attempting to understand the words of Christ must recognize them as spiritual. That requires calling on the Holy Spirit for guidance and support.

There are many scriptures that illustrate both the invisible and visible image of Christ as the Word.

IN THE beginning [before all time] was the Word (Christ),
and the Word was with God, and the Word was
God Himself.
John 1:1 AMP

Before Jesus became flesh He was the substance of God in light and sound. The account of creation in Genesis describes God speaking the substance of all things. When God spoke His Word it released both the light of Christ and life into the material world. For a deeper study on this subject I recommend you read my book *Immersed in Him*. In the book I develop in great detail the method God uses to create "all" things.

All things were made and came into existence through
Him; and without Him was not even one thing made that
has come into being.

In Him was Life, and the Life was the Light of men.

And the Light shines on in the darkness, for the darkness
has never overpowered it [put it out or absorbed it or
appropriated it, and is unreceptive to it].
John 1:3-5 AMP

The life spoken about in the scriptures isn't experienced through our physical light, but within the spiritual light that formed all things. That light, not the one from this world, illuminates the kingdom of God. That's why Jesus told Nicodemus those who are reborn can "see" the kingdom.

Jesus answered and said to him, "Most assuredly,
*I say to you, unless one is born again, **he cannot***
see the kingdom of God. *"*
John 3:3

The eyes and ears of our spirit are the first spiritual senses that both open our understanding and reconnect us to our Heavenly Father. Jesus spoke in parables in order to separate those who had spiritual eyes and hears.

Asked by the Pharisees when the kingdom of God
*would come, He replied to them by saying, **The kingdom***
of God does not come with signs to be observed
or with visible display,
Luke 17:20 AMP

The kingdom of God is invisible to the natural eye and therefore, requires a spiritual rebirth to discern its power and authority. Moreover, it requires courage to resist the fear that floods our unconverted minds. This is the first sign that a battle is underway that's overthrowing your images of security. This is actually good because it drives you to a greater dependency on the Holy Spirit.

As new Believers we all form concepts about Jesus Christ from traditions of man, doctrines and wrong interpretations of the scriptures. Unfortunately, over time we form false beliefs and structures that hinder the work of the Holy Spirit. Many problems eventually surface because our concepts and images have no substance.

Unless we have daily fellowship with Him and revelations of the living Christ, our love and affection for Him will wane.

The Lord told me something that I think is important to share here. "Most people have failed marriages and relationships because they fall "in love" with an image instead of the person. As the image changes over time so does the affection and feelings they "believed" they had for one another."

Human beings are trained at birth to rely on their senses for survival and information.

The mind's complexity learns to store images or pictures in bite-size information like a computer. These digital pictures are historical information and are rarely updated with new information. Therefore, most people go through life responding to people and events with old data. If the image of that person or event doesn't respond the way it was recorded the mind will react negatively. This usually results in conflicts and over time people will either form new images or delete the old data much like a computer.

The same thing can occur with the relationship we form at our first encounter with Jesus. As we said, most attachments are shaped from our preconceived ideas and expectations about people, not from investigating and learning on a continual day-to-day basis. This doesn't only happen in marriages. It also happens to many of those who "fall in love" with Jesus. The encounter is real, but not lasting because they aren't taught to trust His Spirit.

The result is that wrong images are quickly formed by doctrines and generations of wrong teachings. This often leads to bitter disappointment and running from one church to another.

This happens over and over again with those who believe Jesus for their salvation, but are never taught to rely on the Holy Spirit. Unless we intimately "know" the Person of Christ as the kingdom of God we won't surrender to His Lordship as total authority over our lives. This can only be achieved by discovering Him in all His glory, which includes being birthed into Him.

C. Jesus, the Water and the Spirit

Jesus is always speaking about the invisible realm because it's the reality we recognize the instant our spirit is born again.

If we believe the physical realm is reality and the source of our decisions and choices we will follow the same path as the first Adam.

That's why it's critical to be reborn in His Water and Spirit.

The Water and the Spirit are the most essential components of the rebirth experience. Jesus describes Himself as the "living water" to the Samaritan woman at the well. She was just as perplexed as Nicodemus because very few people are acquainted with their true spiritual natures as the source of life. Physical water maintains the physical life, but spiritually we need the water that satisfies all thirsts, Christ Jesus.

For there are three that bear witness in heaven: the Father, the Word, and the Holy Spirit; and these three are one.

And there are three that bear witness on earth: the Spirit, the water, and the blood; and these three agree as one.
1 John 5:7, 8

John understood more about the spiritual realm than any other writer in the scriptures. He spent hours drinking from that living water flowing from the life and words of Jesus. This scripture in 1 John 5 perfectly describes the finished work of the last Adam.

Jesus reconnects heaven and earth. In addition, He redeems mankind with His blood and provides a blessing called the rebirth to those who want to enter Him and His kingdom. It's Jesus, the Water and the Spirit who reconnects us back to our position in the Garden of Eden, now called the kingdom of God.

D. Jesus as the Truth

For the law was given through Moses, but grace
and truth came through Jesus Christ.
John 1:17

Jesus is God's grace, but if we stop there we will remain at the cross waiting for Him to transform us. This is where the gospel of the kingdom begins its demolition on our minds.

There's no gospel of the kingdom without a rebirth and there's no change without the Holy Spirit who is the Spirit of Truth.

*...**the Spirit of truth**, whom the world cannot receive, because it neither sees Him nor knows Him; but you know Him, for He dwells with you and will be in you.*
John 14:17

*But when the Helper comes, whom I shall send to you from the Father, the **Spirit of truth** who proceeds from the Father, He will testify of Me.*
John 15:26

However, when He, the Spirit of truth, has come, He will guide you into all truth; for He will not speak on His own authority, but whatever He hears He will speak; and He will tell you things to come.
John 16:13

Truth is a spiritual force that operates through faith. Truth will expose darkness because truth originates from the heart of God. The Spirit of Truth is the Holy Spirit who is our advocate, helper and prophetic voice. There's no reason or excuse for anyone not to understand the completed work of Christ if they're as serious with that search as they are for the things of this world.

Perhaps you've heard preachers say, "If you know the truth, the truth will set you free?" Then they quickly add Jesus is the Truth.

Jesus is most certainly the Truth, but He's also the Word and what He says in the verses below is rarely quoted.

*Then Jesus said to those Jews who believed Him, "**If you abide in My word**, you are My disciples indeed. **And you shall know the truth, and the truth shall make you free**."*
John 8:31, 32

Jesus is obviously speaking about us leaving this world and entering into Him as the Word. This becomes clear because of His description of a disciple below.

*"**If anyone comes to Me and does not hate his father and mother, wife and children, brothers and sisters, yes, and his own life also, he cannot be My disciple**."*
Luke 14:26

These are His words and they demonstrate that if you and I want to KNOW the Truth we must be born into Him, which is the Word. This is the only way.

I'm sometimes surprised at how easily people are distracted or uninterested in the things that matter for eternity. That's why I'm confident the Spirit of Truth is bringing up a new generation of Believers who won't be denied. They will do whatever it takes to understand the ever-increasing revelations of Christ.

I'm so thankful that I've experienced His grace, but now I want to know the whole truth.

I believe that Truth starts with the glory hidden "in Christ" and it's only experienced after entering His Water and Spirit.

The door to these mysteries begins with the Person of Grace, but most people find that understanding as an encounter with Jesus of Nazareth. That's the Jesus who walked in this earth, but He was transformed into the resurrected Christ, King of Kings and the last Adam.

Therefore, from now on, we regard no one according to the flesh. Even though we have known Christ according to the flesh, **yet now we know Him thus no longer.**
2 Corinthians 5:16

Those who desire Truth must be reborn to see Him the way He really is in His finished work. Mankind, with the mindset of the first Adam – the fallen mind will never get to know Christ because of decisions born from the fear of death.

Those who enter into Christ are set free from the first Adam's mindset and lose their identity and fear of death. Christ's *water* drowns your fears and His Spirit gives you life. That's why the *last Adam* is called the life-giving Spirit.

The conversation between Jesus and Pilate perfectly illustrates that the sound of Truth is neither heard nor understood by those relying on this world.

Pilate therefore said to Him, "Are You a king then?"

Jesus answered, "You say rightly that I am a king.
For this cause I was born, and for this cause I have come
into the world, that I should bear witness to the truth.
Everyone who is of the truth hears My voice."

Pilate said to Him, "What is truth?"
John 18:37-38a

Without a rebirth it's impossible to be led by the Spirit. I'm not saying people won't have experiences with the Holy Spirit because they will. But being led is much different. I now know when my decisions are not "led" by Him, but before being born again I couldn't determine the difference.

We are of God. He who knows God hears us;
he who is not of God does not hear us.
By this we know the spirit of truth and the spirit of error.
1 John 4:6

The spirit of error is made visible through our intimacy with the voice of the Holy Spirit. Once we are born of the Water and Spirit and enter His kingdom our spiritual eyes and ears are opened. The last Adam restored the vision lost by the first Adam in the Garden of Eden.

Jesus answered and said to him, "Most assuredly,
*I say to you, **unless one is born again,***
he cannot see the kingdom of God."
John 3:3

How about you, have your spiritual eyes been reopened? Do you understand that if you aren't seeing the spiritual kingdom of God you haven't unwrapped the rest of your gifts from Christ? He's waiting on you to experience Him as Truth in ways you never knew.

Most Believers today have a poverty mindset. They don't have to live like that because our Heavenly Father is a multi-billionaire. God created everything and God owns everything. But instead of living like sons of the king, they're living like orphans in a slum eating leftovers and not realizing they've been left billions of dollars as their inheritance.

The Bible says that God's people perish for lack of knowledge and it's certainly the case in this example of the poverty mindset.

We've entered a new season on earth that demands a serious discussion of the scriptures and the finished work of Christ. We can't be content any longer with another person's revelation or interpretation of the scriptures.

We must challenge what we believe and why. If we don't, we'll be living from someone else's revelation. We've been designed by God to hear directly from Him. Why would you leave something so important as your eternal destiny in the hands of another?

This book is one of several that I'll be writing in this series to help you find "Truth" for yourselves.

I won't give you a menu of do's and don'ts or another set of doctrines. I will, however, guide you through the Holy Spirit to scriptures that display another dimension of Christ.

We must understand Christ in His fullness, not just His Grace. That journey begins one step at a time as we dismantle our familiarity with a "gospel" and an image that's constructed from this world.

We've grown up with fairy tales and doctrines that have little to do with the reality of the living Christ. Our resistance to the spiritual realm is the result of fear, not faith. The Bible says (paraphrasing) *anything done without faith is sin.*

Sin is the spiritual virus that's nourished by the false belief that death is still ruling over you and this world. Christ destroyed death and if you don't believe that you will live your life as a slave to the imaginary truth and deception that the devil is still in control over this world.

You've now been given the keys to unlock the revelations of Christ for yourself. That journey begins with your submersion into His Water and Spirit. The Holy Spirit is your Guide, Counselor and Advocate into "all Truth." The life you've been waiting to live began before the foundation of the world, but it's not too late to start right now.

CONCLUSION

My deepest desire is that this book and series will challenge you to truthfully assess what you believe and why. This book should quicken a desire inside you to question your personal experience with Christ both as Jesus and as the last Adam.

The ways of God are so mysterious and wondrous that even the angels had no idea what He did. Adam's sin wasn't a surprise, but it was the necessary ingredient God used to trap satan and train future generations to be overcomers.

From Abraham to Jesus, the majestic love story unfolds in so much depth and mystery that the most dramatic feature of Christ's victory has gone unnoticed. _The Last Adam_ describes the kingdom of God on earth now as it was in the beginning when it was called the Garden of Eden. The dominion and power of the first Adam was returned and it's available to those who "violently seize it." The invisible kingdom of God is visible to those born "into" Christ.

Sin is described as anything that's not by faith. But wait, isn't faith the only way to receive the fullness of what Christ has done? That's the beginning of the journey called salvation and that's His gift in the Person of Grace. It's the next step called the "new birth" that requires our greatest efforts, which He measures by our passion and desire.

The "future" most are taught to believe will come actually began the day Christ was resurrected. That's the truth for me and it's the gospel the Holy Spirit instructed me to share with you. What you do with it is up to you. It always has been.

See you in the throne room!

The next book in the series

Who Has Bewitched You?
By: L. Emerson Ferrell

Get your copy today!

VOICE OF THE LIGHT MINISTRIES

WWW.VOICEOFTHELIGHT.COM

Made in the USA
Charleston, SC
20 March 2016